Reducing Your Carbon Footprint on Vacation

Greg Roza

AR B.L.: 8.1 Alt.: 1212
Points: 1.0   MG

Reducing Your Carbon Footprint
on Vacation

Greg Roza

New York

For Heather, Steve, Emily, and Amanda

Published in 2009 by The Rosen Publishing Group, Inc.
29 East 21st Street, New York, NY 10010

Library of Congress Cataloging-in-Publication Data

Roza, Greg.
Reducing your carbon footprint on vacation / Greg Roza.—1st ed.
    p. cm.—(Your carbon footprint)
Includes bibliographical references and index.
ISBN-13: 978-1-4042-1777-5 (library binding)
1. Ecotourism. 2. Sustainable living. 3. Energy conservation. 4. Water conservation.
I. Title.
G156.5.E26R69 2008
640—dc22

                                                                2008003479

Manufactured in the United States of America

On the cover: Left: A hotel utilizes environmentally friendly solar power. Right: Public bicycles are used to reduce congestion and pollution.

Contents

Introduction

Have you ever heard the term "carbon footprint"? Every human being has one, although not everyone understands what it means. It's important for you to understand your carbon footprint and how big it is. The future of our planet may depend on how efficiently the human race can reduce its collective carbon footprint. The only way to accomplish this is for individuals and businesses to work conscientiously and selflessly to reduce their own carbon footprints.

A carbon footprint is a measure of the effect a person or group has on the environment in terms of the greenhouse gases they produce. These effects are measured in units of carbon dioxide—thus the term "carbon footprint." Excess greenhouse gases such as carbon dioxide, methane, and water vapor damage a protective layer of Earth's atmosphere called the ozone layer. This allows more of the sun's energy to reach Earth, causing the temperature of the atmosphere to rise. The rise in temperature causes the melting of Earth's polar ice caps, which reflect much of the sun's heat back into space. In the absence of reflective snow and ice, land and open water absorb more heat from the sun, which increases the temperature of the atmosphere even more.

This cycle is often referred to as global warming. Unless we can put global warming in check now, future generations will undoubtedly encounter increasingly dangerous weather, rising sea levels, desertification, and drought—just to name a few problems.

The term "carbon footprint" refers primarily to the amount of greenhouse gases a person or group of people produces, which affects the rate of global warming. It is usually measured in carbon dioxide emissions produced during a number of daily activities. Your carbon footprint can be broken down into two parts: primary and secondary. Your primary carbon footprint is a measure of the greenhouse gases that you add directly to the atmosphere. Much of an individual's primary carbon footprint comes from the fossil fuels used in transportation and to heat his or her home. Your secondary carbon footprint encompasses all greenhouse gases you contribute indirectly to the atmosphere. This includes the emissions associated with the manufacture, shipping, disposal, and eventual breakdown of products that you purchase or use.

Reducing your carbon footprint means making changes to reduce the amount of carbon dioxide you put into the atmosphere—directly and indirectly. It also means conserving resources (such as paper and water) and avoiding products that are harmful to people and the environment (such as plastics and dangerous chemicals). It can also mean doing what you can to protect the people, cultures, economy, and environment of the communities you visit.

Many people proudly refer to this type of lifestyle as "living green," and it is a trend that's growing more popular every day. There are many things that you as an individual can do to live green and reduce your carbon footprint. In this book, you will learn how to decrease your carbon footprint while on vacation.

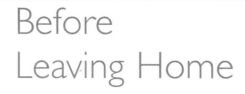

Before Leaving Home

Reducing your carbon footprint while on vacation begins even before you leave your home. By carefully planning where you will stay, how you will travel, and what you will bring with you, you can make your trip as green as possible. It may take more effort and planning, but in the end the environment will thank you.

Researching Your Destination

There are several criteria you should consider when planning an ecologically friendly trip. For example, some modes of transportation are better for the environment than others. Traveling by train is a green way to go, and it can also allow your parents to sit back and watch the scenery instead of worrying about driving. You may want to plan ahead and book hikes and walking tours, which will allow you to avoid car travel once you reach your destination.

When planning a trip to an unfamiliar destination, it is wise to research customs, economy, geography, and wildlife. Understanding the customs of a place will help you to fit in and avoid offending local residents. Researching your destination

This young woman is researching her vacation destination at a local travel agency. Other sources for research include the library, bookstores, and the Internet. There are many magazines dedicated to travel, some of which focus on ecological issues.

will allow you to find green activities such as hikes, wildlife tours, and sightseeing tours. It's also important to know how to behave in a new place in order to protect the local plants and animals. This means you shouldn't litter, take plants from their natural habitats, kill possibly endangered or sacred native animals (bugs included), or buy souvenirs made from local animals. Researching you destination will help you to protect its people and natural resources.

For over fifty years, the Ski Train has been taking vacationers from Denver, Colorado, to Winter Park Resort in the Rocky Mountains. The Ski Train can accommodate up to eight hundred passengers for the 60-mile (96.56 kilometers) trip into ski country.

Once you have chosen a destination, you need to find a green place to stay. Investigate the hotel or bed and breakfast where you intend to stay to be sure that its policies and practices are safe for the environment, or "eco-friendly." You may even choose to patronize a new type of hotel called an eco-lodge. Once you know where you will be staying, you can call ahead to make plans and ask questions about the lodging and the local area.

Plastic Facts

Plastic products are a modern convenience. However, they are also a modern environmental problem. Let's look closely at plastic water bottles, for example. Manufacturing plastic requires oil. According to the Earth Policy Institute, the United States alone uses more than 17 million barrels of oil a year to produce about 29 billion plastic bottles.

Next time you buy a bottle of water, check to see where it was bottled. Chances are the water had to be transported hundreds, perhaps thousands, of miles. This process requires fossil fuels for shipping and refrigeration. According to a 2007 article by Janet Larsen of the Earth Policy Institute, the "annual fossil fuel footprint of bottled water consumption in the United States [is] over 50 million barrels of oil ... enough to run 3 million cars for one year."

According to a 2007 report by the Container Recycling Institute, 52 billion plastic bottles and jugs were wasted instead of recycled in 2005. These plastic bottles will remain in landfills for centuries, polluting our environment with harmful toxins. Even when plastic bottles are disposed of properly in recycling bins, fossil fuels are used for the transportation and processing that recycling requires. When you are traveling, avoid using disposable water bottles. Pack a refillable bottle instead.

What to Pack

When packing for your trip, try to be as environmentally conscious as you can. Don't purchase travel-sized containers of toothpaste, shampoo, deodorant, and so on. These containers—most of which are made of plastic—usually contain just enough product for a few days. Then they

This young man is drinking from a refill-able plastic bottle. This is much better for the environment than disposable water bottles.

are thrown away, and new travel-sized containers are purchased. This increases your carbon footprint due to the amount of fossil fuels required to manufacture, transport, and dispose of the plastic. Instead, reuse containers that you already have, or buy containers that can be refilled every few days.

Pack several cloth tote bags for your shopping purposes when on vacation. This is a better option than receiving plastic bags, paper bags, and Styrofoam when purchasing things. Most of this wasteful packaging is quickly thrown away and dumped in landfills, where it may take thousands of years to decompose. The same goes for food products, like snacks and water. Bring your own reusable water bottle with you, and pack snacks in sealable containers instead of buying snacks wrapped in paper, plastic, Styrofoam, or foil.

Vacation Conservation

While you are away on vacation, electricity still flows through the wires and appliances in your home. Water may drip out of the faucets. The heat will still come on when it gets cold enough. All of these can contribute to a larger carbon footprint. While away on holiday, you can help protect the environment by following the simple steps discussed below.

Unplug

Many appliances require electricity to function. When you turn them on, electricity flows into them from outlets in your home. Did you know, however, that many appliances that are left plugged in draw a small amount of electricity all of the time, even though they are not turned on? Many can draw as much as 40 watts per hour when they are turned off—enough energy to power a typical computer for about ten to fifteen minutes. That may not sound like a lot, but it can add up over time.

Let's say you leave a television—which, when turned off, still draws 40 watts per hour—plugged in while you're on vacation for one week. That is about 6,720 watts of wasted electricity total. Now, let's say you have ten appliances plugged in. That means you have wasted about 67,200 watts of electricity while on vacation. This is enough electricity to keep a typical computer running for about ten days straight. As you can see, unplugging appliances can help keep your electricity bill down, your carbon footprint smaller, and the world a greener place to live.

Turn Down or Turn Off

Some home appliances cannot or should not be turned off or unplugged when you go on vacation. However, many can be set to use less energy than they normally do. Machines that create or reduce heat use the most energy. Air conditioners, for example, are one of the biggest energy hogs in the home. Air conditioners should usually be turned off when no one is home for an extended period of time. A 1,000-watt air conditioner that

The control dial on this hot water heater can be set to "vacation" when leaving the home for a lengthy trip.

runs fifteen minutes for every hour uses 250 kilowatts of energy every hour. If you were to leave this air conditioner on while you were away for twenty-four hours, it would waste 6,000 kilowatts of energy. This would be even worse on a very hot day. Obviously, it is a good idea to unplug or turn off air conditioners while on vacation. If you have animals that will be in the house while you are gone during hot weather, try, instead, to board them with a trusted friend or at a good kennel. If this is not possible, set the air conditioner to a higher temperature than you normally would.

Depending on the time of year, furnaces and heaters should be either turned off or turned down. In warmer weather, this probably won't be an issue; you can just turn your furnace off. In colder weather, home furnaces need to be kept running in order to prevent water pipes from freezing and bursting. When vacationing during the winter, you can turn your thermostat down to 55 degrees—but no lower. This will cut down on the energy you waste while still protecting your home from bursting pipes and flooding. You may also want to turn your water off where it enters the house in order to avoid leaks and burst pipes.

Most water heaters have a "vacation" setting that you can use when you're away for a week or more. If your furnace does not have this function, set the thermostat as low as it will go without actually turning it off. Turning a gas-powered water heater off will cause the pilot light to go out, which may require a professional to relight. If you have an electric water heater, you can cut the electricity to the heater by turning it off or cutting the power at the fuse/breaker box. Other things in the home that should be turned off and unplugged when you are on vacation include VCRs, DVD players, televisions, electric clocks, coffee makers, and computers. All these devices will draw electricity if they are plugged in, even if they are turned off.

Stop the Presses!

One more thing that you should "turn off" is your newspaper subscription. A week of unread newspapers is a lot of wasted paper. It takes energy to print and transport newspapers. Suspending your subscription while on vacation will help reduce your carbon footprint. If you can't cancel the paper, you may be able to donate that week's worth of papers to a local school or library.

2 Traveling Green

With limited time for a vacation, it is difficult to travel long distances without booking a flight on an airplane. Once you reach your destination, it may be tricky to get around without using an automobile. People who are concerned about the environment, however, work to find ways to avoid airplane and automobile travel whenever they can.

Automobiles and the Environment

A car that travels eighteen miles to and from work five times a week, forty-eight weeks a year, creates about 4,500 pounds of carbon dioxide, 160 pounds of carbon monoxide, and 16 pounds of nitrogen oxide. Today there are about seven hundred billion cars on the world's roads. They produce about 2.8 billion tons of carbon dioxide a year. This amounts to about 20 percent of the world's carbon dioxide emissions. Car exhaust also contains hydrocarbons, which are molecules that contain hydrogen and carbon and contribute greatly to global warming.

The environment is not only damaged by car exhaust but also by everything that has sprung up to support car travel— automobile plants, car dealerships, roads, highways, and

A passenger jet comes in for a landing at Los Angeles International Airport over a heavily congested highway. This is a common scene in cities all over the world, and it contributes greatly to the already high levels of greenhouse gases added to the atmosphere every year.

junkyards. The more automobiles traveling in an area, the more damage to the environment and the more resources that are wasted. It should be easy to see that avoiding automobile travel while away from home will help you to reduce your carbon footprint.

Airplane Travel and the Environment

There are far more automobiles on the road than there are airplanes in the sky, but air travel as a whole produces nearly twice as much greenhouse gases per mile per passenger than other forms of intercity travel.

Jet engines release carbon dioxide directly into the upper atmosphere during flights. They actually increase ozone in the layer of Earth's atmosphere called the troposphere. Although this form of ozone does not last very long, it is a greenhouse gas that contributes greatly to global warming. In addition, jet contrails (streams of water vapor) are also believed to negatively affect Earth's climate.

A plane releases harmful carbon dioxide and nitrogen oxide as it lands and takes off, taxis on the runway, and idles in preparation for the next flight. Airports usually attract heavy automobile traffic into and out of them, which only adds to the pollution. In addition, the construction and maintenance of terminals and roads leading to them has a negative impact on the local environment and atmosphere.

Airlines use a wide variety of paper, plastic, and Styrofoam products. Meal trays, food wrappers, plastic cups, and even in-flight magazines increase the amount of garbage that is produced by airlines. Tens of thousands of trees are cut down to make paper airline tickets each year.

This reduces the number of trees removing carbon dioxide from the atmosphere. Furthermore, the production and delivery of these products used by the airlines require the burning of fossil fuels.

Public and Alternative Transportation

When used by many people, public transportation saves energy and reduces pollution. According to the American Public Transportation Association Web site, public transportation produces 95 percent less carbon monoxide and about half as much carbon dioxide and nitrogen oxide per passenger mile compared to private vehicles.

Each item in this airline meal—including the plastic utensils—comes sealed in plastic wrappers and foil trays, which are bad for the environment.

Some people choose to vacation closer to home in order to reduce their carbon footprint. Shorter plane or car rides mean a smaller carbon footprint. Others choose to take a local vacation—they opt to see sites that are close to home that they've never seen before. Sometimes, these options aren't available to you, especially when you want to take a vacation far from home. Still, there are ways for you to reduce your carbon footprint, even when air travel is necessary. There are also ways to avoid car travel once you have reached your destination.

The Brienz Rothorn Bahn (BRB) is a steam locomotive. It has been taking travelers from the city of Brienz, Switzerland, to the top of Brienzer Rothorn mountain since 1892. The BRB is a great way to reduce your carbon footprint on your way to an exciting vacation getaway.

Trains

Europe and Asia are well known for their extensive railway systems that allow travelers to go from country to country in comfort and ease. Some trains make stops in rural areas as well. Large cities sometimes have light rail trains and subways that take you where you need to go locally. The train systems in the United States and Canada are not as extensive as those in Europe and Asia, but you can still travel to many interesting locations on both local and long-distance lines. Many train travelers love to sit back and read a book, watch the scenery pass by, or take a nap while the train does all the hard work.

Comfort and ease aren't the only reasons to travel by train. Much like automobiles and airplanes, many trains burn fossil fuels—particularly diesel fuel—that release carbon dioxide into the atmosphere. However, trains generally release less than half as much carbon dioxide per passenger than cars do. Many modern trains run at least partly on electricity. Some use 100 percent electrical power to function. Still others use power-

Tour buses can be a great way to sit back and enjoy the local scenery. This open-top bus stops by the beautiful Alum Bay on the Isle of Wight in England.

ful magnets to propel a train at great speeds. In addition, modern trains release very little carbon monoxide. The more people who start taking the train instead of flying or driving, the healthier our planet will be.

Buses

Buses burn fossil fuels just like automobiles do. However, some scientists estimate that a bus with as few as seven passengers is more fuel-efficient than a car carrying one person. A bus emits about 80 percent less carbon monoxide per mile than a car does. In addition, many fleets of buses today no longer use gasoline. Some use a type of fuel called biodiesel. Other buses use hydrogen cells as a fuel source.

Boats

While traveling by ship might take longer in many instances than other forms of transportation, it can be a very relaxing and beautiful way to travel. It is also better for the environment than driving or flying. In some cases, traveling by boat can result in a shorter trip compared to driving or flying. For example, the Staten Island Ferry in New York City is the busiest passenger ferry service in the world. It is often a quicker way than driving to get from Staten Island to Manhattan and back in a city known for its congested streets.

When You Absolutely Must Fly

Even when you absolutely must fly, there are ways to help reduce your carbon footprint. First, when in the airport or on the airplane, try to avoid buying drinks in plastic bottles, food in Styrofoam trays, unnecessary paper products, magazines, and newspapers. All of these products contribute greatly to your carbon footprint because they require fossil fuels for production and transportation. If you can, bring your own snacks and drinks in reusable containers.

Book flights with airlines that recycle the waste created when serving food and beverages to passengers. British Airways, for instance, has very strong environmentally friendly policies. Southwest Airlines recycles all cabin waste. Most airlines offer online tickets, or e-tickets, instead of paper tickets. Research airlines before flying to make sure that the one you choose is doing something to offset the damage its planes are doing to the atmosphere.

British Airways and Carbon Offsetting

There is only so much an airline can do to reduce its carbon footprint, given that, currently, all jet engines burn fossil fuels. Some airlines, however, have begun to take a strong environmental stance in the hope of making a difference. British Airways has embarked on an especially aggressive environmental campaign known as carbon offsetting, or carbon trading.

Carbon offsetting is a way of mitigating, or softening, the effect of one's carbon footprint. For example, when someone needs to book a flight on an airplane, he or she may contribute a portion of the ticket price to the planting of trees. The trees are meant to offset or make up for the negative effects of the flight. A person who does this is said to be carbon neutral for that trip.

British Airways has taken this concept to the corporate level. In 2007, for example, it was a member of an international conference on business travel that was held in Barcelona, Spain. To offset the carbon dioxide released during the planning and execution of the conference, British Airways sponsored a program in the state of Karnataka, India, to replace that area's dependence of fossil fuels with the use of more eco-friendly biofuels. The biofuels are produced locally, which created many jobs for local people. British Airways has led the airline industry in carbon offsetting for more than seven years.

When You Absolutely Have to Drive

Many people ride share and carpool when commuting to work on a daily basis. Sharing rides when on vacation can also help reduce your carbon footprint. If you and a group of friends are taking a road trip, avoid taking

Three friends carefully pack their car while preparing for a road trip. Ride sharing can be more cramped than taking separate vehicles, but it is better for the environment.

more than one vehicle if you can. You might even decide to rent a larger vehicle to transport numerous people. The fewer vehicles you take on vacation, the better it is for the environment.

If you want to drive to your vacation spot, consider buying or renting an automobile that is more fuel-efficient than most cars. Some cars now run on gasoline alternatives that are better for the environment, like biodiesel. Hybrid vehicles are better for the environment because they use two different systems to create power—usually a traditional combustion engine and an electric motor. Together, these two systems help reduce the fuel a car burns. Cars with fuel cells use hydrogen and oxygen to create electricity. The only by-products of a fuel cell are heat and water.

On Vacation

Choosing more "green" forms of transportation is just one way to reduce your carbon footprint while away from home. Once you have reached your vacation destination, there are many ways for you to continue protecting our planet from harm.

Getting Around on Vacation

Do what you can to avoid automobile and plane travel while on vacation. If you are in a city, familiarize yourself with the bus and subway systems there. Many hotels and airports offer shuttle services. If you are in a rural area or other natural setting, enquire about buses, trains, shuttles, and ferries.

Whenever possible, walk when you are on vacation instead of using a car or taking a cab or bus. Not only is walking excellent for the environment, it is also good for your health. You will gain a more intimate understanding of the local area, and you might even come across hidden, out-of-the-way sights you might not have seen had you taken a vehicle. Many hotels and vacation packages offer guided tours and hikes of the local area. Or, ask your hotel for a map of the local area and explore it for yourself. This will allow you to get an up-close

Vélib', which means "free bicycle" or "bicycle liberty," is a public bicycle rental program in Paris, France.

look at the hot spots while reducing your carbon footprint.

Some cities have a bicycle-share program that you may be able to use to get around town. Once again, this will allow you to get an up-close understanding of your destination, improve your health, and protect the environment—all at the same time. A number of ambitious bicyclists even like to take cycling vacations. This option could turn out to be the greenest and most exciting vacation you've ever had.

Going Green in Your Hotel Room

Thanks to a growing worldwide concern for the state of the environment, choosing a green place to stay while on vacation is becoming easier than ever before. Some hotels specifically cater to environmentally concerned travelers. Many are starting to change their policies based on the requests of their guests, so don't be afraid to speak up and tell them that you want to help the environment. Most hotels and inns will gladly accommodate you, regardless if it is a "green" hotel or not, for fear of losing your business.

When you check into a hotel, notify the management that it is not necessary to change your towels and sheets every day. This will

Dominica is an island nation in the Caribbean Sea. The 3 Rivers Eco-Lodge is an environmentally friendly resort in the beautiful, secluded rainforest of Dominica. Travelers can enjoy clean rivers, peaceful accommodations, and beautiful beaches.

reduce the amount of energy needed to launder them. Take shorter showers in order to reduce the amount of energy used to heat the water. Bring your own soaps, shampoos, and other toiletries to avoid using the small, plastic-packaged toiletries that most hotels provide. Some eco-friendly hotels supply refillable bulk containers of shampoo, conditioner, soap, and lotions in their rooms. This cuts down on the amount of plastic used and reduces the work hotels need to do to prepare rooms for guests.

Green Vacation at Lake Powell

Lake Powell is a human-made reservoir on the border between Utah and Arizona. It was created when the Glen Canyon Dam was finished in 1963, flooding the Glen Canyon and forming an artificial lake. The Glen Canyon National Recreation Area has become a popular vacation destination for many Americans over the past few decades. Many people enjoy camping, fishing, and boating there. Some even like to rent a houseboat for an extended stay on Lake Powell.

Reducing Lake Powell's carbon footprint is very important to the people who run and maintain Glen Canyon National Recreation Area. In 2001, the area's electricity use was reduced by 500,000 kilowatts, and water use was reduced by 1,215,780 gallons. The Glen Canyon staff has worked hard to conserve resources and clean up litter. In 2006, Lake Powell Resorts & Marinas recycled 27 tons of paper, which is enough to save 357 trees. Those trees help to reduce the amount of carbon dioxide in our atmosphere. Many other resorts and hotels are also doing what they can to help the environment. If you are trying to reduce your carbon footprint, Lake Powell would be a great place to vacation.

Avoid ordering food through room service, which usually comes with paper napkins, plastic cutlery, cups, lids, and wrappers. Instead, bring your own food in reusable containers, or give your business to local restaurants. If your hotel provides glasses in your room, use them instead of plastic cups, which often come wrapped in yet another layer of plastic. Don't make coffee or tea with in-room coffeemakers and supplies. Grab a cup at a nearby café instead. This allows you to support local businesses while avoiding the disposable cups, stirrers, filters, and foil wrappers that come with the coffee in your room. It also cuts down on the amount of electricity that you use. If you must use items provided in your rooms, recycle and reuse them.

To avoid wasting electricity, don't leave chargers for electronic devices plugged in when you are not using them. Rather than throwing newspapers and magazines away when you are done with them, leave them in the lobby for other guests to read or ask the front desk where you can recycle them. Let hotels know that you plan to check out electronically, if they offer that service, so you can cut down on paper tickets and receipts. Finally, when leaving your room for the day and at checkout, turn off the air-conditioning, heat, lights, and television to cut down on wasted electricity.

Green Eating

By researching your destination, you can find environmentally friendly restaurants, markets, and shops to patronize. Hotel employees can give you information about local restaurants and markets. Avoid fast-food restaurants because they create tons of paper and plastic waste.

Bring your own utensils and cloth napkins with you when traveling. This is much better than using a plastic fork and a paper napkin for a quick meal and then throwing them away. Bring refillable coffee cups, water bottles, and travel mugs for drinks. Bring your own containers for leftovers instead of using containers provided by restaurants. Whenever

Most tourist destinations, such as Grand Canyon National Park in Arizona, provide recycling receptacles. Always recycle your garbage on vacation to help reduce your carbon footprint.

possible, purchase fresh vegetables and make you own salads, rather than purchasing foods packaged in plastic, paper, and Styrofoam.

At every opportunity, select foods that were grown or produced in the local area. The ships, trucks, and trains used to transport food contribute to greenhouse gas emissions. The farther the food travels, the worse it is for the environment.

Out and About

It is hard to avoid plastic consumption while traveling, but do what you can. Refill water bottles from taps and fountains. Reject plastic bags and containers as often as possible. Bring your own tote bags for shopping. Never litter while on vacation, and never throw anything out of the windows of a moving vehicle. Depending on what you throw away, your litter can pollute the streets or countryside in different ways. Save your garbage for a garbage can, and recycle and reuse what you can. Also, don't forget that someone else will probably have to clean up after you, which raises the cost of cleaning and maintaining an area.

This woman uses a solar-powered battery charger while on a bicycle trip with her family.

Most vacationers need batteries to power electronic devices such as cameras, radios, MP3 players, and flashlights. When left in junkyards, however, batteries can break down and release harmful chemicals into the environment. The packages that batteries come in are made of paper and plastic. Batteries are shipped all over the world, increasing the amount of greenhouse gases emitted into the atmosphere. Purchase rechargeable batteries for your electronic devices. This will reduce battery waste. There are also solar battery rechargers now, which will reduce the amount of electricity you use.

The best way to reduce your carbon footprint is to purchase electronic equipment with rechargeable batteries already installed. Use a digital camera if possible. The processing of film and development of pictures requires the use of toxic chemicals that get poured down the drain and back into the water supply. In addition, used film canisters end up in landfills and take hundreds, if not thousands, of years to decompose. Never use disposable cameras. If you have to buy film, buy rolls with the highest amount of exposures.

4 Becoming an Ecotourist

Reducing your carbon footprint is a noble and important endeavor in our increasingly fragile world. As you have read, "going green" may require some difficult and not-so-difficult changes in your life. But the benefits far outweigh the relatively minor hardships and sacrifices. You have learned many valuable tips on how to reduce your carbon footprint while away from home—these are things that all of us can do. The sooner we start practicing them, the better off our planet and all its inhabitants will be.

More and more people in our world are priding themselves on their concern for natural environments and protecting local ways of life. Because of their efforts, a new term has been coined in recent years: ecotourism. Ecotourists are a cross between hardcore travelers and truly concerned environmentalists.

Much of ecotourism is based on the concept of sustainable travel, or leaving the world in the same—or better—shape than before you went on vacation. It requires that we seriously think about the greenest ways to get from one place to another. It also means respecting the local area, people, wildlife, customs, and culture. Caring about sustainable travel does not mean that your vacation will be less fun. On the contrary, it can make your vacation the most exciting and fulfilling one you have ever taken.

There is no concrete definition for the term "ecotourism." Depending on whom you ask, the answers may differ. However, most ecotourists agree on the basic ideas of traveling green. Ecotourism revolves around people and businesses that develop policies to protect natural environments, help local communities, educate travelers about the importance of reducing their carbon footprints, and encourage travelers to educate others about sustainable travel. Businesses that participate in ecotourism—especially hotels and resorts—are sometimes called "eco-lodges." These places are committed to conservation, education, and improving the lives of local residents. Ecotourists must adhere to rules established by eco-lodges and concerned organizations that have made it a priority to establish the standards of sustained travel and ecotourism.

Eco-Lodges

The main aim for hotels and businesses participating in ecotourism is minimizing the impact travel and vacationing have on the environment while protecting and promoting local businesses, cultures, and customs. They practice ecologically friendly activities, many of which were addressed in chapter 3. However, eco-lodges take green practices to the extreme. Not only do they conscientiously reduce their own carbon footprints in any way possible, they also make it a priority to build environmental awareness in their clientele. In addition to taking steps to protect the environment, businesses that participate in sustainable

In Shompole, Kenya, local workers construct buildings for a new eco-lodge. Ecotourism efforts in the area have helped reduce poverty, improve commerce, and repopulate the region's wildlife.

travel provide financial assistance to conservation associations and local community groups.

Cultural respect is just as important as environmental awareness. Just as eco-lodges work to educate people about the environment, they also educate travelers about the social, political, cultural, and economic standards of the surrounding community. Eco-lodges help protect and improve the well-being of the local environment and people. This can be accomplished in many ways. Most eco-lodges offer donations to worthwhile charities, help repair town and village structures, and contribute to or head up beautification projects.

Some lodges are locally owned and operated, and they are the best businesses to visit. Non-native eco-lodge owners and workers can support the health of the local economy by hiring local residents. Restaurants and hotels serve regional foods, which helps out local farmers, green markets, and grocery stores. In this way, eco-lodges strive to provide an enjoyable experience for both visitors and locals.

Ecotourists

As previously mentioned, ecotourists give careful consideration to the items they pack, purchase, and use—for instance, no plastic water bottles, no gas-guzzling SUVs, and no Styrofoam. Ecotourists always use public transportation or walk. They take only one map or brochure for the entire group they are traveling with in order to cut down on paper consumption.

Ecotourists never litter or deface property with graffiti. When touring a natural setting, they take with them everything they brought in. In fact, most make it a practice to pick up litter that has been left by others

The city of Puerto Princesa, Philippines, has implemented an annual Valentine's Day mangrove tree planting for ecotravelers. The program helps strengthen the local environment, improves the local economy, and provides travelers the chance to immerse themselves in the local culture.

wherever they go. When camping, hiking, or on a tour, they follow the local rules. Ecotourists stay on marked trails, do not chop down trees for firewood, and try to leave the area just as they found it when they arrived.

To be a good ecotourist, research the local plants and animals before selecting a destination. Educate yourself on which animals are considered pests and which are respected by local people. This will allow you to avoid killing insects and small creatures that are actually beneficial to the environment or revered by locals. Ecotourists prefer to

Travelers view wildlife from an observation cabin in Scotland. Many ecotourists enjoy viewing and taking photos of birds and other animals instead of purchasing souvenirs.

"hunt" plants and animals with binoculars and cameras. Don't purchase souvenirs made from local plants and animals, especially those that are made with materials from endangered creatures. Such materials include tortoise shells, ivory, and hides. Many animals are hunted just to make these products for tourists.

Much like eco-lodges, ecotourists give as much consideration to the local people and culture as they do to the local environment. When traveling to an unfamiliar place, always research the local customs and

The Seven Principles of "Leave No Trace"

Leave No Trace is an international association concerned with educating travelers about how they can reduce their carbon footprints and overall impact on the environment. The following list contains the Seven Leave No Trace Principles, which are based on scientific research and common sense:

- Plan ahead and prepare.
- Travel and camp on durable surfaces.
- Dispose of waste properly.
- Leave what you find.
- Minimize campfire impacts.
- Respect wildlife.
- Be considerate of other visitors.

manners. This will help you to avoid coming across as arrogant or inadvertently offending anyone. Go out of your way to meet and befriend the people, learning as much about them as you can. Ecotourists accept that people and cultures can be different and unfamiliar, and they appreciate a chance to learn about diversity.

Many ecotourists enjoy the surprises they discover while exploring local stores, markets, museums, and theaters. The money you give to these businesses bolsters the local economy. Avoid shopping at tourist shops, since they are often owned by those who are based outside the community or even the country. The money you spend in such stores rarely stays in the community. Likewise, stay at local hotels instead of large motel chains, whose headquarters are usually in another city or country. Experiment with local foods and purchase locally made products whenever possible.

Spread the Word

Now that you know all about reducing your carbon footprint when you're on vacation, perhaps you, too, will become an ecotourist. Make a pledge to give your vacation dollars to organizations and businesses that have environmentally friendly programs and policies. Let "green" companies know you approve of the way they do business.

There is much you can do locally to help educate others about the importance of sustainable travel and ecotourism. Write letters to politicians, hotel managers, bus companies, airlines, and associations explaining why reducing our collective carbon footprint is a crucial issue. Contribute time and money to conservation groups. Teach others the importance of sustainable travel and respecting local wildlife, people, and customs. By spreading the word about our carbon footprint and leading by example, we might be able to protect our planet and all the creatures that call it home.

Glossary

biodiesel A renewable fuel for diesel engines that is made from natural oils, like soybean oil.

carbon monoxide A colorless, odorless, toxic gas that is formed when carbon-containing compounds are burned in a space characterized by a lack of air.

combustion engine An engine, like those found in most cars, that burns fossil fuels in order to create energy.

commute To travel regularly from one place to another, particularly between home and work.

diesel A thick, oily fossil fuel used in many large vehicles.

endangered In danger of ceasing to exist.

environmentalist Someone involved in issues relating to the protection of the natural world.

fuel cell A device that generates electricity by converting chemical energy to electric energy.

greenhouse gas A gas that contributes to the warming of Earth's atmosphere by reflecting heat and light from Earth's surface.

methane A colorless, odorless, flammable gas that is used as a fuel.

nitrogen oxide A product of burning fossil fuels and greenhouse gas.

ozone A form of oxygen with three oxygen atoms per molecule. Ground-level ozone is a pollutant, but ozone in the upper atmosphere helps block harmful rays from the sun.

patronize To be a customer of a particular store or business.

reservoir A large lake used for collecting and storing water for human use.

souvenir Something bought or kept as a reminder of a place or occasion.

Styrofoam A light, plastic material that is used to make disposable items, like cups and packing materials.

synthetic Artificial or human-made.

troposphere The lowest and most dense layer of the atmosphere.

watt A standard unit of electrical power.

For More Information

Container Recycling Institute
1776 Massachusetts Avenue NW, #800
Washington, DC 20036
(202) 263-0999
Web site: http://www.container-recycling.org
A nonprofit organization founded in 1991 that researches and promotes policies that
reduce the production and increase the recycling of plastic bottles and other
containers.

Earth Day Canada
111 Peter Street, Suite 503
Toronto, ON M5V 2H1
Canada
(888) 283-2784
Web site: http://www.earthday.ca
An association devoted to educating Canadian citizens about environmental issues
and encouraging them to make positive changes.

Green Hotels Association
P.O. Box 420212
Houston, TX 77242-0212
(713) 789-8889
Web site: http://www.greenhotels.com
An association committed to promoting environmentally conscious travel, especially
through encouraging hotels to implement green practices.

The International Ecotourism Society (TIES)

1333 H Street NW, Suite 300E

Washington, DC 20005

(202) 347-9203

Web site: http://www.ecotourism.org

The world's largest ecotourism association promotes responsible travel to natural areas and is a global source of information about ecotourism.

Leave No Trace (LNT)

P.O. Box 997

Boulder, CO 80306

(800) 332-4100

Web site: http://www.lnt.org

A nonprofit organization dedicated to educating people worldwide about the responsible enjoyment and active stewardship of the outdoors.

Pembina Foundation for Environmental Research and Education

Box 7558

Drayton Valley, AB T7A 1S7

Canada

Web site: http://www.pembinafoundation.org

The Pembina Foundation is dedicated to environmental research for the purpose of educating people about the production and use of energy and its impact on our world.

Sustainable Travel International

P.O. Box 1313

Boulder, CO 80306

(720) 273-2975

Web site: http://www.sustainabletravelinternational.org

This nonprofit organization promotes sustainable and responsible travel through programs that encourage consumers, businesses, and travel-related organizations to contribute to the environmental, cultural, and economic values of the places they visit.

Web Sites

Due to the changing nature of Internet links, Rosen Publishing has developed an online list of Web sites related to the subject of this book. This site is updated regularly. Please use this link to access the list:

http://www.rosenlinks.com/ycf/onva

For Further Reading

Bishop, Amanda. *How to Reduce Your Carbon Footprint.* New York, NY: Crabtree Publishing, 2008.

Cherry, Lynne. *How We Know What We Know About Our Changing Climate: Scientists and Kids Explore Global Warming.* Nevada City, CA: Dawn Publishing, 2008.

Elliot, Marion. *Fun with Recycling: 50 Great Things for Kids to Make from Junk.* Lanham, MD: Southwater, 2001.

Harlow, Rosie. *Garbage and Recycling.* Boston, MA: Kingfisher, 2002.

Langholz, Jeffrey, and Kelly Turner. *You Can Prevent Global Warming (and Save Money!): 51 Easy Ways.* Kansas City, MO: Andrews McMeel Publishing, 2003.

Povey, Karen D. *Biofuels.* Farmington Hills, MI: KidHaven Press, 2006.

Royston, Angela. *Travel of the Future.* Portsmouth, NH: Heinemann, 2007.

Thornhill, Jan. *This Is My Planet: The Kids' Guide to Global Warming.* Toronto, ON: Maple Tree Press, 2007.

Trask, Crissy. *It's Easy Being Green: A Handbook for Earth-Friendly Living.* Layton, UT: Gibbs Smith, 2006.

Bibliography

American Public Transportation Association. "Public Transportation: Benefits for the 21st Century." Retrieved January 7, 2008 (http://www.apta.com/research/info/online/twenty_first_century.cfm).

Arkansas Department of Environmental Quality. "Cars and Air Pollution." Retrieved January 5, 2008 (http://www.adeq.state.ar.us/default.htm).

Association of Corporate Travel Executives. "Successful Carbon Neutral Initiative to Expand." March 28, 2007. Retrieved January 8, 2008 (http://www.acte.org/resources/press_release.php?id=146).

British Airways. "Carbon Trading and Offsetting." Retrieved January 8, 2008 (http://www.britishairways.com/travel/csr-carbon-trading/public/en_gb).

Brower, Michael, and Warren Leon. *The Consumer's Guide to Effective Environmental Choices: Practical Advice from the Union of Concerned Scientists*. New York, NY: Three Rivers Press, 1999.

David, Laurie, and Cambria Gordon. *The Down-to-Earth Guide to Global Warming*. New York, NY: Orchard Books, 2007.

Gershon, David. *Low Carbon Diet*. Woodstock, NY: Empowerment Institute, 2006.

Gitlitz, Jennifer, and Pat Franklin. "Water, Water Everywhere: The Growth of Non-Carbonated Beverages in the United States." Container Recycling Institute. February 2007. Retrieved January 3, 2008 (http://www.container-recycling.org/assets/pdfs/reports/2007-waterwater.pdf).

GreenLearning.ca. "Climate Change Solutions: Lifestyle." Pembina Foundation. Retrieved January 7, 2008 (http://www.greenlearning.ca/climate/solutions/lifestyle/2).

Higham, James. *Critical Issues in Ecotourism: Understanding a Complex Tourism Phenomenon*. Burlington, MA: Butterworth-Heinemann, 2007.

Hoffman, Andrew J. *Carbon Strategies: How Leading Companies Are Reducing Their Climate Change Footprint*. Ann Arbor, MI: University of Michigan Press, 2007.

Honey, Martha. *Ecotourism and Sustainable Development: Who Owns Paradise?* 2nd edition. Washington, DC: Island Press, 2008.

Horn, Greg. *Living Green: A Practical Guide to Simple Sustainability*. Topanga, CA: Freedom Press, 2006.

Larsen, Janet. "Bottled Water Boycotts: Back-to-the-Tap Movement Gains Momentum." Earth Policy Institute. December 7, 2007. Retrieved January 3, 2008 (http://www.earth-policy.org/Updates/2007/Update68.htm).

Leave No Trace. "Seven Principles of Leave No Trace." Retrieved January 7, 2008 (http://www.lnt.org/programs/principles.php).

Patterson, Carol. *The Business of Ecotourism*. Victoria, BC: Trafford Publishing, 2007.

Project Better Place. "Project Better Place: Fact Sheet." Retrieved January 5, 2008 (http://www.adeq.state.ar.us/AIR/ozone/cars.htm).

Rogers, Elizabeth, and Thomas M. Kostigen. *The Green Book: The Everyday Guide to Saving the Planet One Simple Step at a Time*. New York, NY: Three Rivers Press, 2007.

Spence, Christopher. *Global Warming: Personal Solutions for a Healthy Planet*. New York, NY: Palgrave MacMillan, 2005.

Weaver, David B. *The Encyclopedia of Ecotourism*. Wallingford, England: CABI, 2003.

Index

About the Author

Greg Roza has written and edited educational materials for children for the past eight years. He has a master's degree in English from the State University of New York at Fredonia. Roza enjoys camping and traveling with his family and participating in outdoor activities. He lives in Hamburg, New York, with his wife, Abigail, and his three children, Autumn, Lincoln, and Daisy.

Photo Credits

Designer: Les Kanturek; Photo Researcher: Amy Feinberg